The Crowd is Untruth

(Annotated) with Meditations and Scriptures

by Soren Kierkegaard
Annotations by Aaron Whitehead

Table of Contents

The Crowd is Untruth

by

Soren Kierkegaard

On the Dedication to

"That Single Individual" [1]

Translated by Charles K. Bellinger

Annotations and Meditations by Aaron Whitehead

Introduction

*Do you not know that in a race all the runners run,
but only one gets the prize? Run in such a way as to
get the prize. - 1 Corinthians 9:24*

My dear, accept this dedication; it is given over, as
it were, blindfolded, but therefore undisturbed by
any consideration, in sincerity. Who you are, I
know not; where you are, I know not; what your
name is, I know not. Yet you are my hope, my joy,
my pride, and my unknown honor.

It comforts me, that the right occasion is now there
for you; which I have honestly intended during my
labor and in my labor. For if it were possible that
reading what I write became worldly custom, or
even to give oneself out as having read it, in the
hope of thereby winning something in the world,
that then would not be the right occasion, since, on
the contrary, misunderstanding would have
triumphed, and it would have also deceived me, if I
had not striven to prevent such a thing from
happening.

This, in part, is a possible change in me, something
I even wish for, basically a mood of soul and mind,
which does not produce change by being more than
change and therefore produces nothing less than
change; it is rather an admission, in part a

thoroughly and well thought-out view of "life," of "the truth," and of "the way."

There is a view of life which holds that where the crowd is, the truth is also, that it is a need in truth itself, that it must have the crowd on its side. [2] There is another view of life; which holds that wherever the crowd is, there is untruth, so that, for a moment to carry the matter out to its farthest conclusion, even if every individual possessed the truth in private, yet if they came together into a crowd (so that "the crowd" received any decisive, voting, noisy, audible importance), untruth would at once be let in. [3]

First Meditation

Kierkegaard says his reflections are "a thoroughly and well thought-out view of "life," of "the truth," and of "the way." This is a reference to John 14:6 where Jesus says that He is "the way", "the truth" and the "life". According to Kierkegaard, his reflections are bringing us into a deeper view of Jesus. Spend a moment and ask the Holy Spirit to guide you through your reading and meditation into a deeper knowledge of Jesus as the way, the truth, and the life.

"There is a view of life which holds that where the crowd is, the truth is also". How have you seen this in your own life? Have you ever held this view? Have you agreed with "the crowd" and allowed it to dictate what you thought was truth? Take a moment and ask the Lord for forgiveness for those areas in your life where you have compromised real truth with the views of "the crowd".

Only One Receives the Prize

For "the crowd" is untruth. Eternally, godly,
Christianly what Paul says is valid: "only one
receives the prize," [I Cor. 9:24] not by way of
comparison, for in the comparison "the others" are
still present. That is to say, everyone can be that
one, with God's help - but only one receives the
prize; again, that is to say, everyone should
cautiously have dealings with "the others," and
essentially only talk with God and with himself - for
only one receives the prize; again, that is to say, the
human being is in kinship with, or to be a human
is to be in kinship with the divinity.

The worldly, temporal, busy, socially-friendly
person says this: "How unreasonable, that only one
should receive the prize, it is far more probable that
several combined receive the prize; and if we
become many, then it becomes more certain and
also easier for each individually." Certainly, it is far
more probable; and it is also true in relation to all
earthly and sensuous prizes; and it becomes the
only truth, if it is allowed to rule, for this point of
view abolishes both God and the eternal and "the
human being's" kinship with the divinity; it
abolishes it or changes it into a fable, and sets the
modern (as a matter of fact, the old heathen) in its
place, so that to be a human being is like being a
specimen which belongs to a race gifted with

reason, so that the race, the species, is higher than the individual, or so that there are only specimens, not individuals. But the eternal, which vaults high over the temporal, quiet as the night sky, and God

in heaven, who from this exalted state of bliss, without becoming the least bit dizzy, looks out over these innumerable millions and knows each single individual; he, the great examiner, he says: only one receives the prize; that is to say, everyone can receive it, and everyone ought to become this by oneself, but only one receives the prize.

Where the crowd is, therefore, or where a decisive importance is attached to the fact that there is a crowd, there no one is working, living, and striving for the highest end, but only for this or that earthly end; since the eternal, the decisive, can only be worked for where there is one; and to become this by oneself, which all can do, is to will to allow God to help you - "the crowd" is untruth.

Second Meditation

"Only one..." Kierkegaard takes away the idea of being a part of the crowd to "receive the prize". Even going so far as to say that where many work the goal can be only earthly, because only the individual can work towards what is eternal. Are you counting on being counted among those in your church? Do you consider your association with your church to be your "saving grace"? The Lord wants you. Take a moment, in silence, and present yourself before God. No associations. No affiliations. Just you. Allow the Lord to speak directly to you.

"God in heaven, who from this exalted state of bliss, without becoming the least bit dizzy, looks out over these innumerable millions and knows each single individual". Allow this thought to sit in your mind. Among these "innumerable millions", He knows you. In Matthew 10:29-31, Jesus says, "Are not two sparrows sold for a penny? Yet not one of them will fall to the ground apart from the will of your Father. And even the very hairs of your head are all numbered. So don't be afraid; you are worth more than many sparrows."

A Crowd

A crowd - not this or that, one now living or long
dead, a crowd of the lowly or of nobles, of rich or
poor, etc., but in its very concept [4] is untruth,
since a crowd either renders the single individual
wholly unrepentant and irresponsible, or weakens
his responsibility by making it a fraction of his
decision. Observe, there was not a single soldier
who dared lay a hand on Caius Marius; this was
the truth. But given three or four women with the
consciousness or idea of being a crowd, with a
certain hope in the possibility that no one could
definitely say who it was or who started it: then
they had the courage for it; what untruth!

The untruth is first that it is "the crowd," which
does either what only the single individual in the
crowd does, or in every case what each single
individual does. For a crowd is an abstraction,
which does not have hands; each single individual,
on the other hand, normally has two hands, and
when he, as a single individual, lays his two hands
on Caius Marius, then it is the two hands of this
single individual, not after all his neighbor's, even
less - the crowd's, which has no hands. In the next
place, the untruth is that the crowd had "the
courage" for it, since never at any time was even the
most cowardly of all single individuals so cowardly,
as the crowd always is.

For every single individual who escapes into the
crowd, and thus flees in cowardice from being a
single individual (who either had the courage to lay
his hand on Caius Marius, or the courage to admit
that he did not have it), contributes his share of
cowardice to "the cowardice," which is: the crowd.
Take the highest, think of Christ - and the whole
human race, all human beings, which were ever
born and ever will be born; the situation is the
single individual, as an individual, in solitary
surroundings alone with him; as a single individual
he walks up to him and spits on him: the human
being has never been born and never will be, who
would have the courage or the impudence for it;
this is the truth. But since they remain in a crowd,
they have the courage for it - what frightening
untruth.

Third Meditation

The cowardliness of a crowd "renders the single individual wholly unrepentant and irresponsible, or weakens his responsibility by making it a fraction of his decision". How many wars or battles have started where no one knows who fired the first shot? Ney's cavalry charge at Waterloo? The Boston Massacre? The "Shot heard round the world" at Lexington? Much of Nazi Germany and the power of Hitler came from the deindividuation of groupthink. In the context of a crowd, individual responsibility is lost. Do you allow yourself to hide in a crowd? Do you "go with the flow" even when it's wrong? Are you taking responsibility for your actions?

Those Who...Lead the Crowd

The crowd is untruth. There is therefore no one who has more contempt for what it is to be a human being than those who make it their profession to lead the crowd. Let someone, some individual human being, certainly, approach such a person, what does he care about him; that is much too small a thing; he proudly sends him away; there must be at least a hundred. And if there are thousands, then he bends before the crowd, he bows and scrapes; what untruth!

No, when there is an individual human being, then one should express the truth by respecting what it is to be a human being; and if perhaps, as one cruelly says, it was a poor, needy human being, then especially should one invite him into the best room, and if one has several voices, he should use the kindest and friendliest; that is the truth. When on the other hand it was an assembly of thousands or more, and "the truth" became the object of balloting, then especially one should god-fearingly - if one prefers not to repeat in silence the Our Father: deliver us from evil - one should god-fearingly express, that a crowd, as the court of last resort, ethically and religiously, is the untruth, whereas it is eternally true, that everyone can be the one. This is the truth.

Fourth Meditation

Who are those who lead the crowd? Are you sending away those who are "too small" and welcoming the multitudes?

Jesus taught in Matthew 25, "whatever you did for one of the least of these brothers and sisters of mine, you did for me" (v. 40). Let us strive to welcome all into our "best room" and speak with our "kindest and friendliest" voices to those who are counted among the "least of these".

Therefore was Christ Crucified

The crowd is untruth. Therefore was Christ crucified, because he, even though he addressed himself to all, would not have to do with the crowd, because he would not in any way let a crowd help him, because he in this respect absolutely pushed away, would not found a party, or allow balloting, but would be what he was, the truth, which relates itself to the single individual. And therefore everyone who in truth will serve the truth, is in some way or other a martyr; if it were possible that a human being in his mother's womb could make a decision to will to serve "the truth" in truth, so he also is a martyr, however his martyrdom comes about, even while in his mother's womb.

For to win a crowd is not so great a trick; one only needs some talent, a certain dose of untruth and a little acquaintance with the human passions. But no witness for the truth - alas, and every human being, you and I, should be one - dares have dealings with a crowd. The witness for the truth - who naturally will have nothing to do with politics, and to the utmost of his ability is careful not to be confused with a politician - the god-fearing work of the witness to the truth is to have dealings with all, if possible, but always individually, to talk with each privately, on the streets and lanes - to split up the crowd, or to talk to it, not to form a crowd, but so that one or another individual might go home from the assembly and become a single individual.

"A crowd," on the other hand, when it is treated as the court of last resort in relation to "the truth," its judgment as the judgment, is detested by the witness to the truth, more than a virtuous young woman detests the dance hall. And they who address the "crowd" as the court of last resort, he considers to be instruments of untruth. For to repeat: that which in politics and similar domains has its validity, sometimes wholly, sometimes in part, becomes untruth, when it is transferred to the intellectual, spiritual, and religious domains. And at the risk of a possibly exaggerated caution, I add just this: by "truth" I always understand "eternal truth." But politics and the like has nothing to do with "eternal truth." A politics, which in the real sense of "eternal truth" made a serious effort to bring "eternal truth" into real life, would in the same second show itself to be in the highest degree the most "impolitic" thing imaginable.

Fifth Meditation

We live in a society of busyness. Rushing here and there in our air-conditioned cars, isolated us from the elements and each other, our interactions with others have moved to the place of mindless exchanges. Dealing with people we are often tempted to think of others in a general sense; them, those I have to engage with simply because they cross my path. We pull into our garages, shut the doors, and close ourselves into a fortress of seclusion.

In living in this way, though feigning individuality, we are in fact confronting everyone we meet as a part of the crowd. Kierkegaard offers that "the god-fearing work of the witness to the truth is to have dealings with all, if possible, but always individually, to talk with each privately, on the streets and lanes". The value is in the individual. Make an effort to engage with those you meet, who cross your path "on the streets and lanes", on an individual level, truly seeking to recognize the value which they possess as an individual and as a child of God.

Our Age's Misery

The crowd is untruth. And I could weep, in every case I can learn to long for the eternal, whenever I think about our age's misery, even compared with the ancient world's greatest misery, in that the daily press and anonymity make our age even more insane with help from "the public," which is really an abstraction, which makes a claim to be the court of last resort in relation to "the truth"; for assemblies which make this claim surely do not take place.

That an anonymous person, with help from the press, day in and day out can speak however he pleases (even with respect to the intellectual, the ethical, the religious), things which he perhaps did not in the least have the courage to say personally in a particular situation; every time he opens up his gullet - one cannot call it a mouth - he can all at once address himself to thousands upon thousands; he can get ten thousand times ten thousand to repeat after him - and no one has to answer for it; in ancient times the relatively unrepentant crowd was the almighty, but now there is the absolutely unrepentant thing: No One, an anonymous person: the Author, an anonymous person: the Public, sometimes even anonymous subscribers, therefore: No One. No One! God in heaven, such states even call themselves Christian states. One cannot say that, again with the help of the press, "the truth" can overcome the lie and the error. O, you who say this, ask yourself: Do you dare to claim that human beings, in a crowd, are just as quick to reach for truth, which is not always palatable, as for untruth, which is always deliciously prepared, when in addition this must be combined with an admission that one has let oneself be deceived! Or do you dare to claim that "the truth" is just as quick to let itself be understood as is untruth, which requires no previous knowledge, no schooling, no discipline, no abstinence, no self-denial, no honest self-concern, no patient labor!

No, "the truth," which detests this untruth, the only goal of which is to desire its increase, is not so quick on its feet. Firstly, it cannot work through the fantastical, which is the untruth; its communicator is only a single individual. And its communication relates itself once again to the single individual; for in this view of life the single individual is precisely the truth. The truth can neither be communicated nor be received without being as it were before the eyes of God, nor without God's help, nor without God being involved as the middle term, since he is the truth. It can therefore only be communicated by and received by "the single individual," which, for that matter, every single human being who lives could be: this is the determination of the truth in contrast to the abstract, the fantastical, impersonal, "the crowd" - "the public," which excludes God as the middle term (for the personal God cannot be the middle term in an impersonal relation), and also thereby the truth, for God is the truth and its middle term.

Sixth Meditation

Kierkegaard's reaction in this section shows his distrust of "the press" because of its ability to allow a person to be anonymous in their expression of their feelings and opinions. In his opinion allowing for a lack of accountability, and therefore, a lack of truth. Kierkegaard died in 1855, long before the invention of the internet.

Consider how the presence of the internet in our society extends the ability to be anonymous even farther. We must fight the temptation to remain anonymous and live with integrity and sincerity. Take a moment and reflect on Psalm 139. Make this your prayer for today, "Search me, O God, and know my heart; test me and know my anxious thoughts. See if there is any offensive way in me, and lead me in the way everlasting."

Honor Every Individual Human Being

And to honor every individual human being, unconditionally every human being, that is the truth and fear of God and love of "the neighbor"; but ethico-religiously viewed, to recognize "the crowd" as the court of last resort in relation to "the truth," that is to deny God and cannot possibly be to love "the neighbor." And "the neighbor" is the absolutely true expression for human equality; if everyone in truth loved the neighbor as himself, then would perfect human equality be unconditionally attained; every one who in truth loves the neighbor, expresses unconditional human equality; every one who is really aware (even if he admits, like I, that his effort is weak and imperfect) that the task is to love the neighbor, he is also aware of what human equality is.

But never have I read in the Holy Scriptures this command: You shall love the crowd; even less: You shall, ethico-religiously, recognize in the crowd the court of last resort in relation to "the truth." It is clear that to love the neighbor is self-denial, that to love the crowd or to act as if one loved it, to make it the court of last resort for "the truth," that is the way to truly gain power, the way to all sorts of

23

temporal and worldly advantage - yet it is untruth; for the crowd is untruth.

Seventh Meditation

Matthew 22:36-40 - [36] "Teacher, which is the greatest commandment in the Law?" [37] Jesus replied: "'Love the Lord your God with all your heart and with all your soul and with all your mind.' [38] This is the first and greatest commandment. [39] And the second is like it: 'Love your neighbor as yourself.' [40] All the Law and the Prophets hang on these two commandments."

When Jesus is asked about the commandments he says that loving God and neighborhood are the crux of the Law. Kierkegaard's point here is that, in loving our neighbor, we are expressing "the truth and fear of God". For in honoring those around us we realize their equality with us. We are all children of God. Therefore, we ought to love them as ourselves. This love may often be "weak and imperfect", but the action is needed just the same. May this be your prayer today: "Lord, help me to love You with all my heart, with all my soul, and with all my mind. And may You teach me to love and honor my neighbor, even as I love and honor myself. Amen"

Conclusion

But he who acknowledges this view, which is seldom presented (for it often happens, that a man believes that the crowd is in untruth, but when it, the crowd, merely accepts his opinion en masse, then everything is all right), he admits to himself that he is the weak and powerless one; how would a single individual be able to stand against the many, who have the power! And he could not then want to get the crowd on his side to carry through the view that the crowd, ethico-religiously, as the court of last resort, is untruth; that would be to mock himself.

But although this view was from the first an admission of weakness and powerlessness, and since it seems therefore so uninviting, and is therefore heard so seldom: yet it has the good feature, that it is fair, that it offends no one, not a single one, that it does not distinguish between persons, not a single one. A crowd is indeed made up of single individuals; it must therefore be in everyone's power to become what he is, a single individual; no one is prevented from being a single individual, no one, unless he prevents himself by becoming many.

To become a crowd, to gather a crowd around oneself, is on the contrary to distinguish life from life; even the most well-meaning one who talks about that, can easily offend a single individual. But it is the crowd which has power, influence, reputation, and domination - this is the distinction of life from life, which tyrannically overlooks the single individual as the weak and powerless one, in a temporal-worldly way overlooks the eternal truth: the single individual.

Final Meditation

There can be no way for Kierkegaard's argument to take root. If a large group of people were to agree with it, they would make a crowd. And a crowd, as he has said, is untruth. It would be hypocritical, then, to seek for the crowd to acknowledge what it is by nature; that is, untruth. And yet, this contradiction is exactly what also gives the argument its power. For every crowd is made up of individuals and each individual can think for himself and recognize the truth, found in individuality. The power of the crowd is lost, then, when each individual realizes who they are.

As with Kierkegaard's argument, our weaknesses can frequently become our greatest strengths. In 2 Corinthians 12:9 God says His "power is made perfect in weakness". When we accept our struggles and weaknesses we admit our need for help. This gives room for God to work through us in such a way that only He can get the glory. There is no way we could have the power, strength, wisdom, or knowledge to accomplish such a task. Take a moment in silence and allow God to reveal to you areas in your life where He can use your weaknesses to bring Him glory. Strive to live in your weaknesses so that He can fully live in you. Then truly you can say, like Paul in Philippians 4:13, "I can do everything through him who gives me strength."

Note to the Reader

Note: The reader will recall, that this (the beginning of which is marked by the atmosphere of its moment, when I voluntarily exposed myself to the brutality of literary vulgarity) was originally written in 1846, although later revised and considerably enlarged.

Existence, almighty as it is, has since that time shed light on the proposition that the crowd, seen ethico-religiously as the court of last resort, is untruth. Truly, I am well served by this; I am even helped by it to better understand myself, since I will now be understood in a completely different way than I was at the time, when my weak, lonely voice was heard as a ridiculous exaggeration, whereas it can now scarcely be heard at all on account of existence's loud voice, which says the same thing.

Biblical References

1 Corinthians 9:24 - Do you not know that in a race all the runners run, but only one gets the prize? Run in such a way as to get the prize.

John 14:6 - Jesus answered, "I am the way and the truth and the life. No one comes to the Father except through me."

Psalm 139
For the director of music. Of David. A psalm.

1   O Lord, you have searched me and you know me.
2   You know when I sit and when I rise; you perceive my thoughts from afar.
3   You discern my going out and my lying down; you are familiar with all my ways.
4   Before a word is on my tongue you know it completely, O Lord.
5   You hem me in—behind and before; you have laid your hand upon me.
6   Such knowledge is too wonderful for me, too lofty for me to attain.
7   Where can I go from your Spirit? Where can I flee from your presence?
8   If I go up to the heavens, you are there; if I make my bed in the depths, you are there.

9   If I rise on the wings of the dawn, if I settle on the far side of the sea,

10   even there your hand will guide me, your right hand will hold me fast.

11   If I say, "Surely the darkness will hide me and the light become night around me,"

12   even the darkness will not be dark to you; the night will shine like the day, for darkness is as light to you.

13   For you created my inmost being; you knit me together in my mother's womb.

14   I praise you because I am fearfully and wonderfully made; your works are wonderful, I know that full well.

15   My frame was not hidden from you when I was made in the secret place. When I was woven together in the depths of the earth,

16   your eyes saw my unformed body. All the days ordained for me were written in your book before one of them came to be.

17   How precious to me are your thoughts, O God! How vast is the sum of them!

18   Were I to count them, they would outnumber the grains of sand. When I awake, I am still with you.

19   If only you would slay the wicked, O God! Away from me, you bloodthirsty men!

20   They speak of you with evil intent; your adversaries misuse your name.

21   Do I not hate those who hate you, O Lord, and abhor those who rise up against you?

22   I have nothing but hatred for them; I count them my enemies.

23   Search me, O God, and know my heart; test me and know my anxious thoughts.

24   See if there is any offensive way in me, and lead me in the way everlasting.

Footnotes

[1] This, which is now considerably revised and enlarged, was written and intended to accompany the dedication to "that single individual," which is found in "Upbuilding Discourses in Various Spirits." Copenhagen, Spring 1847.

[2] Perhaps, however, it is right to note once and for all, that which follows of itself and which I have never denied, that in relation to all temporal, earthly, worldly ends the crowd can have its validity, even its validity as a decisive court of last resort. But I am not speaking about such things, which I pay so little attention to. I speak of the ethical, the ethical-religious, of "the truth," and seen ethico-religiously the crowd is untruth, when it is taken as a valid court of last resort for what "the truth" is.

[3] Perhaps, however, it is right to note, although it seems to me to be almost superfluous, that it naturally could not occur to me to object to something, for example that there is preaching, or that "the truth" is proclaimed, even though it was to an assembly of a hundred thousand. No, but even if it were an assembly of just ten - and if there should be balloting, that is, if the assembly were the court

of last resort, if the crowd were the decisive factor, then there is untruth.

[4] The reader will therefore recall, that here by "crowd," "the crowd" is understood as a purely formal conceptual definition, not what one otherwise understands by "the crowd," when it supposedly is also a qualification, when human selfishness irreligiously divides human beings into "the crowd" and the nobles, and so forth. God in heaven, how would the religious arrive at such inhuman equality! No, "crowd" is the number, the numerical; a number of noblemen, millionaires, high dignitaries, etc. - as soon as the numerical is at work, the "crowd" is "the crowd."

Made in the USA
Columbia, SC
12 November 2020